I SPY
SOCCER

CAN YOU GUESS ALL THE PUZZLES?
LET'S SEE!

I SPY WITH MY LITTLE EYE SOMETHING BEGINNING WITH..

a is for

(Captain's) Armband

I SPY WITH MY LITTLE EYE SOMETHING BEGINNING WITH...

b is for

Ball

I SPY WITH MY LITTLE EYE SOMETHING BEGINNING WITH...

C is for

Corner Flag

I SPY WITH MY LITTLE EYE SOMETHING BEGINNING WITH..

d is for

Dribble

I SPY WITH MY LITTLE EYE SOMETHING BEGINNING WITH..

 **is for**

Field

I SPY WITH MY LITTLE EYE SOMETHING BEGINNING WITH..

g is for

Goalkeeper

I SPY WITH MY LITTLE EYE SOMETHING BEGINNING WITH..

h is for

Header

I SPY WITH MY LITTLE EYE SOMETHING BEGINNING WITH..

i is for

Injury

I SPY WITH MY LITTLE EYE SOMETHING BEGINNING WITH..

j is for

Jersey

I SPY WITH MY LITTLE EYE SOMETHING BEGINNING WITH...

l is for

Linesman Flag

I SPY WITH MY LITTLE EYE SOMETHING BEGINNING WITH...

m is for

Medal

I SPY WITH MY LITTLE EYE SOMETHING BEGINNING WITH..

n is for

Net

I SPY WITH MY LITTLE EYE SOMETHING BEGINNING WITH..

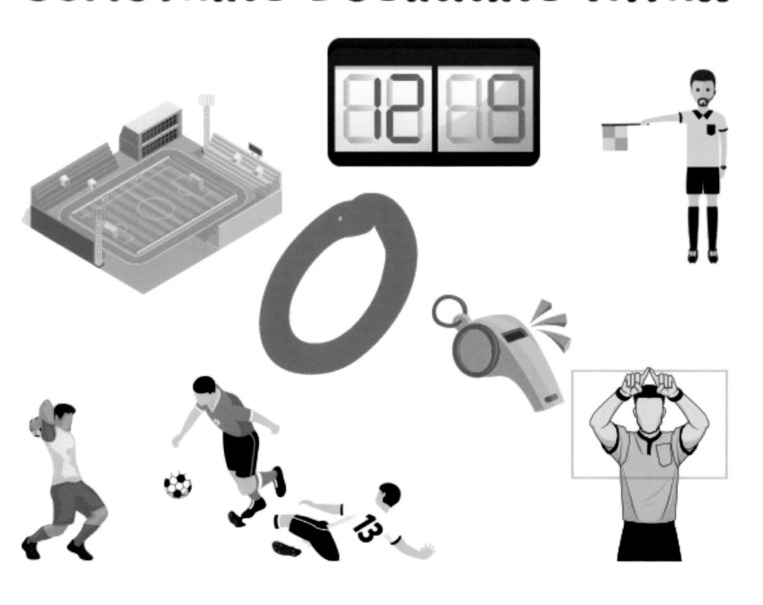

 is for

Offside

I SPY WITH MY LITTLE EYE SOMETHING BEGINNING WITH..

P is for

Penalty Kick

I SPY WITH MY LITTLE EYE SOMETHING BEGINNING WITH...

 **r** is for

Referee

I SPY WITH MY LITTLE EYE SOMETHING BEGINNING WITH...

S is for

Scoreboard

I SPY WITH MY LITTLE EYE SOMETHING BEGINNING WITH..

t is for

Throw-in

I SPY WITH MY LITTLE EYE SOMETHING BEGINNING WITH..

V is for

Var
(Video Assistant Referee)

I SPY WITH MY LITTLE EYE SOMETHING BEGINNING WITH..

 **W** is for

Whistle

I SPY WITH MY LITTLE EYE SOMETHING BEGINNING WITH..

Y is for

Yellow Card

Manufactured by Amazon.ca
Bolton, ON